Shifting Seasons
A Collection of Poetry

Michelle Julian

Shifting Seasons

Copyright © 2025 Michelle Julian

ISBN 979-8-218-57872-5 (paperback)
ISBN 979-8-218-57876-3 (e-book)

All rights reserved. No part of this book may be reproduced, scanned, or transmitted in any form, digital or printed, without the written permission from the author.

Cover art by April Julian

For updates on the author, visit @michellejuliann Via Instagram

Introduction

Poetry has been my therapy—a way to visualize, express, and transform my emotions into something that feels both raw and healing.

Reading the works of others has often helped me feel seen, understood, and less alone. That's what I hope this book can offer you.

This book moves through five chapters: Euphoria, the bliss of first love; Dissonance, the undoing of that perfect image; Unraveling, where anxiety and depression take hold; Transition, the slow and imperfect practice of healing; and Renewal, finally emerging stronger—changed, but whole.

Table of Contents

EUPHORIA	1
DISSONANCE	10
UNRAVELING	19
TRANSITION	28
RENEWAL	46

EUPHORIA

In the first moment of time we shared, our souls leapt out of our bodies to shake hands again.

Innocent smiles hide parallel timelines.

Even before I met you, we had shared a kiss once, in our life before.

You've come to see me!

I've been waiting for you.

I'm charmed by your mystique, my Middlemist red.

Your presence ignites this fire in me, and I burn at your feet.

Now, my heart jumps at your soft grays and blues—hues I once overlooked, now visible in the light of our years, deepening the love I carry for you.

White noise fills my ears,
making my vision sparkle
and my mind hush.

This buzzing noise blocks
all shame living in me
while you're caressing my
body.

Your textured voice and
warm sighs make my aura
gush.

This invisible force bursting
between us—completely
pure.

You put a flower in my
hair in the park, in our
hometown, where we first
met.

I watch those memories,
the sparkle in our eyes,
clearly blissful, so distant.

Vast,

beyond the ordinary, you
can feel the beauty in our
admiration.

I see it now—the string
that pulls us through our
story, making wrong turns
and attempting to knot up
today.

Seeing you feels like a
whisper in the crowd,
telling me I'm safe.

Thin black lines, some
don't notice, but they
box us in.

Your words are alive as
they move through me
and form to my body.

I plead with my eyes,
praying my touch is like
a magnet.

So desperate as you
hold me—my body
goes limp.

Watching from the
future, all I see is a girl,
naive in your presence.

A boy of spontaneity, you showed me how to free my mind!

I fell for your knowledge and your shifted gaze—our futures outlined.

Every time I turned a new stone, it delighted me, and I used each one as building blocks for my own path.

Thank you! I cry now, remembering the shaping stories we were told but did not listen to.

Was it bold?

The tears of our past now terrorize our future, but I know we will surpass it; just show me new stones to turn, ones I couldn't have seen without your eyes next to mine.

A Message to My Mind:

I can see you, screaming I've done something wrong.

I can't hear you, anymore.

Your voice is faint.

Have I danced with my heart for too long?

I'll have to start again, relearn your language, before I lose you altogether.

DISSONANCE

Haze consumes me, dripping down my *raw skin*.

What a fine line we walk between a dream and fate.

My head pounds, vibrating the boat.

Still, we float hand in hand through endless streams, so familiar and free.

What's it going to be?

The continuation of our merged lives grows green and breaks through the strongest ice each winter.

Still, we hesitate.

At night, she hears the scream, the
one that keeps her from sleeping.

In the dark, she searches hard for
the light that lines their past.

Her pupils are huge; she swims
in the dark, and it swallows her
whole.

Fragment by fragment, the light
dims low.

Her soul fades and she continues
to look until the light diminishes.

She will swim forever, looking for
a reason to stay.

Peeling back your layers nauseates
my soul. Grimacing truth scraping my
skull—tearing apart the new—shredding
all meaning.

Clean air consumes my lungs for once!
Now I see clearly. I am relieving these
chains, free of poison, free to forgive.

Knowledge of the ugly truth offers the
gift of sight, the ability to see the beauty
within myself I so often overlook.

Your facade outshines my power no
more.

What a mind trick.

Time ticks; my shoulders rise; my body runs its own timeline.

Lack of progress feeds self-loathing.

Then,
I race to find the right path. I'm incomplete! I fill and fill hoping my cup will overflow, but then I'm left to clean it up myself!

Then,
slowly I fade away,
trying to catch my breath
while notes pound loudly
throughout my brain.

I can't sleep these days, figuring out new ways to become self-made. Anger consumes me as if it was a poison made just for me.

Still,
I choose to drink it without an antidote. Now I'm arrogantly picking fights—I hurt deep and strive for a new path.

I'm sorry I took it out on you.

The room is rejecting my shape.

The cold is consuming my lungs.

I shrink at the light.

My arms grip my torso—the only barrier I have left.

As the darkness closes in on me, I'm glad I can feel the pain and not the everlasting hollow halls of emptiness.

Those rooms are so dark.

The beauty begged to be seen, but
was barely heard through the noise.

Her worth was clouded by a narrow
vision. She stood still in the crowd,
waiting to be noticed, carrying a
chest full of life.

She dwindled; the night crawled in
and choked her out.

She awaited the day she could use
her light to fill a room again.

We awe at the shape
until we are qualified to
color outside of the lines.

Trying new turns idle—
we are deemed a fool.

We must circle back.

At the door, you whisper my name.

My body runs toward the sound,
only to find a ghostly entrance.

Knives run through my blood,
searching for my heart.

I continuously dip into my past as
if it won't poke and poke at me.

UNRAVELING

The devil prances on my mind,
creeping around as the winter
does on each fallen leaf.

This devil of mine paints a
star so bright, just to destroy it
before my eyes, for each night
I watch it's fatal demise, I'm
reminded of time.

All night I weep, not for the
fallen soldiers, precisely, that's
a feeling I have yet to endure.

However, I drown in the
melodies offered by this evil,
contrasting the world we both
adore.

I believe he keeps me sharp in
this brutal space.

I can never remember the first
night we met. But since then,
I've known evil in this life and
my opinions grew bold.

Grudges

She sits alone
on the train
as workers go
by.

She receives a
letter, stuffed
with anger,
sealed by a
smile-shaped
stamp.

She opens the
poor letter
and drinks
the *poison*.

As we all do.

The wound is so fresh I can't breathe.

The stitching is still raw. It's agony staring at my white, plain ceiling.

Sharp pieces of my broken heart shred through my lungs.

I can't breathe.

Ego

He creeps up on me throughout my lifetime, crushing my breath in moments of glory, tugging on the back of my head, pulling my soul out from under me to starve my creativity.

Over and over, I face the
same problems—each
with a different face.

How much longer until I
learn my lesson? I want to
see how good it can get.

The face is stored on the shelf—a
saint to be admired, laughing and
crying at the sounds of the winds
eroding away at its life.

It sits still and never complains.

A curated image—built of many
opinions—changing only by force.

But, once it lived purely on its
own intuition. Until the world
passed it by—on to the next.

A single word can be scripture;
to each their own value.

Lists of memories flood my eyes,
turning my gaze red.

Lists of memories, awaiting my
stamp of approval so it can be
released.

I once waited for your approval,
for your words to fill me.

I used to glow vibrant with life, and now I see a stranger in my reflection.

Why am I the one who is lost now? For a moment, the breeze in the car swallows my pain, eclipsing my thoughts. I wait for the light to blind me, even for a small moment.

The lack of your presence pains me, haunting my eternity.

I'll find you in the crevices of my mind one day, just waiting to be seen again.

Until then, I'll treasure any minute that conceals the fatigue my heart suffers while healing.

TRANSITION

I've fallen to absurd voids.

A gap that served my ego,
I've filled it with debris.

I dug and dug at the aged
fragments, each one begged
to be let free.

The patterns smiled at me,
consumed my soul, and
exclaimed insights.

My bewildered cycles of
life and growth dilated my
perspective every time a leaf
turned.

So, I let them fall further
and buried my past beneath.

Naive baby, you fell down a rabbit hole.

You were so young and hopeful, yet powerless over your own strength. You let people dress you; their visions obsessed you. How could you see clearly when you didn't even want to?

I see now why you dug graves of shame and learned to survive by saying what they wanted to hear.

Oh, but wasn't it fun?

To have played this version you thought meant "adult." The party and drugs—all to impress. It removed the pressures, the pressures to be all-new, not the real you.

The fun years now feel like nightmares. All that trouble led you so far off your path, but only through the chaos could you discover your truest form.

And for that, I thank you.

The love was there; we lived off it!
But so was the ignorance.

Unable to mold the excitement into
a solid foundation, we threw our
passion at each other instead,
expecting a house to form.

Her heart drowns in poison.
A dark aura clings to her presence.

She faces each day at 40%, then wonders why her dreams don't match her reality.

How breaking a moment could be for those in places not truly aligned with their souls.

Expectations:

An all-consuming fog raining on the notion of who I could become.

These large fields of subjective territory are becoming too difficult to comb through.

Surely, I'll pluck the weeds, and maybe recognizing them will become easier with time.

I hope the fog clears soon.

I used to dream of the lure of night, and each time it pulled me in, I agreed.

The street lamp turns and the sun sets. Bones smirk at the energy shift while demons crawl into the minds of tainted visions.

I lost myself to the ghosts many times; it was exciting then.

Now I postpone the ghosts.

I need a guard.

The angels sing in my ears each night to protect me as I walk the streets alone.

I beg the demons for forgiveness.

To My Distant Cousin

Even when I'm lost, I can feel you with me.

Even though we live separate lives, we have seen the same ghosts.

With our shared history, are our minds somehow connected? Could we have similar epiphanies, sparked by ancient castles built with our ancestor's tears—turmoil we have never seen but somehow hear?

They whisper guidance into our lives, a voice we have come to call intuition.

Curious bird
bouncing around
           able to feel
           this hateful world.

Singing the song
my mother knew
           telling the stories
           made to heal.

I can see where I am supposed to be.

I fill my world with things that should help me grow.

Is it all for show?

The bright lights feel like everyone is moving while I'm just waiting.

The world passes by, and I'm hurting. I keep wondering, when will my time come?

My thumb pressed against shiny metal,
purchased to hug the bones on my finger,
filling my void with sensations of worth,
pseudo accomplishments.

I used to tell myself my belongings made
me superficial.

Subjective.

They can represent more than the product
itself. They represent the money I worked
hard for and used to bring a new object
into my life.

My persona exclaims facts about me to
new people, constructed by these objects.

It all adds to my story.

Running in circles—I'm beat. I'm drawing out figures; because I need a reason. I figure out meaning too late, then the era claims erasure.

These years feel longer. She said they'd be shorter. I race to the end. "Slow down," they said.

Still,
I race to the end.
I can't help it.

Dark shields form over my eyes. A glaze I can only feel. Screen after screen, you'd think I'd burn out; instead, I learned to process it quicker.

Out in public these pretty smiles haunt me, telling me I've got to sharpen up. Song after song, like a chapter in my head, showing me what I am not.

All the noise—what it takes!

All becomings, while I comb the possibilities.

It feels like I'm dissolving; I know it is essential.

I've longed for a different version of myself, a "better" version. But I didn't know how painful it would be to dissolve the present me.

My ego screams every waking moment, prowling my dreams.

The good days make it worth it. But I'm dying for this to end.

Cinder blocks and chains tie my
soul to this adaptation of hell,
and the speakers play their voice
over and over, telling me that it
was all a choice in the end.

Most things are.

My shadow wishes to punish,
but why be the tortured and
torturer?

Believe in nuances, run from
cycles, and the light will lift you
out.

A kind word can be a
surprise these days. The
faintest tap to the heart
and a sigh of relief.

We dance to sterile
rhythms all in the name
of normalcy.

A kind word can seem
out-of-tune these days.
Can't be real; must be
fake.

Hatred is too often the
tempo in society, so
are those kind words a
reality or just assimilated
personalities?

Never mind negative
assumptions, it's
important to believe in
the lasting magically
effect a kind word can
have, genuine or not.

I've been sitting here, burning
through repeated ideas and
tending to an old cut I barely
feel anymore.

It drags me down, sitting in
despair with so much to look
forward to, especially knowing
I have a choice to progress.

I will now shift my perspective.

If I look for the light in my life,
I will notice the sun comes out
when we sleep. Flowers bloom
in each of the cracks. Hugs drag
us back home.

I find the time to heal.

I received the energy from the sun much more as a child.

I felt its power course through my veins and fuel my soul.

I avoided the energy that day—unintentionally—hoping to find it elsewhere.

I had years when I allowed myself to pause and receive effortlessly. No shadows tailed behind me.

The warmth ever so slightly lifted the corners of my mouth and expanded my chest.

Next time, I'll remember.
For now, I just miss her.

Flowers

The physical presence
of its being demands it's
space as its essence sings
in the higher dimensions.

It gracefully waves at us,
acting so content with it's
placement in the world,
you can't help but to look
at it in awe.

It whispers lullabies to me
in the park.

Slowing my breath, I
finally listen intently.

"Slow down," they beg.

RENEWAL

Down by the beach, salty gusts of wind painted my future in the distance.

How sweet...

to be kissed by a star and caressed by the sand.

At the beach, my mind

                        went

                                  silent.

I finally heard my dreams.

I flew into a place
      that washed away
           with every waking thought.

Now, I always chase it.

If time is a social construct, it
can easily skew your journey
to the top of your mountain.

Everyone learns to take
a vertical path; to use the
railing the wise have laid out
so carefully.

Moving horizontal
                      is unacceptable.

It becomes impossible to
dream past the checkpoints
tethered to our paths.

If you learn the language of
your soul, it can free you and
grant you peace.

I have new experiences stealing my clean slate—how exciting!

Still, the Old World twists my imagination, and my wrinkled values weigh on my endeavors, leaving me indecisive.

I stand here now as both a reflection of my past and a vessel for my future.

No matter how comfortable I feel resting in my wins, I will embrace sudden change.

I believe in making room for dreams I have not yet imagined, slithering into my mind.

Pull away those
pressing ideals. Peel
off the tacky layers.

It takes courage
to scoop meaning
into life, seemingly
never-ending, for
the knowledge you
spread becomes the
foundation of those
who will miss you.

Days have been hitting me
hard, but it enables my soul.

So often I feel my soul dance
around to its wonderful tunes
while I spend an obnoxious
amount of time trying to fix
my mind.

When I do listen to my soul
and decide to dance with her,
my mind quiets.

Finally.

I see the green light luring me
towards my purpose.
I let flushed dreams take my
focus.

For a few moments, all is free.

The sureness in the voice of art
drags me down softly.

I can't help but to listen to it.

Only at her will do I dance
freely.

I get a chill when the world
touches me.

My fingertips buzz at the
soft whispers of every voice
that has lived before me and
around me.

Ideas float above us, waiting
to be pulled in by your own
magnetism.

They talk and talk, first as
whispers, but then the levels
grow, loud and bold, until
it's impossible not to catch it.

This hill becomes quite lonely
in the afternoons, as I daydream
you sitting here with me.

How painful it is to forget the
power of independence.

I decide to let myself blossom.

I pull the strings I need to forgive.

I gather what strength is left and
dive in.

I'll fill my cup on my own now
and see myself in a pretty light.

Hopefully, the next time
I imagine your face, it is
unrecognizable.

This new chapter is creeping up on me, jumping with intent and dancing into my conversations.

I can feel my sorrow shifting to a new rhythm, preparing my heart to open back up.

I've seen this road before, it's patterns understood only by my soul and the carvings she carries.

My heart constructs a radiant warmth, glowing through my eyes, attracting new opportunities into my life.

Every night, I dream of this—an angelic aura taking shape, a life full of truth and purpose.

I keep my eye on Ms. Future.
I know she exists.

She talks to me sometimes.

I see her.

Some days, I am beginning
to feel her presence.

Guide me.

I don't want to lose any
hope this time.

Reading has the power to freeze time, just as music can lighten a room.

People crave stories—especially those they can see themselves in.

Relating to a story turns the thoughts in their heads—all cluttered and often confusing, into something meaningful.

Always make time to create.

Always.

www.ingramcontent.com/pod-product-compliance
Lightning Source LLC
LaVergne TN
LVHW061049070526
838201LV00074B/5228